WASHINGTON

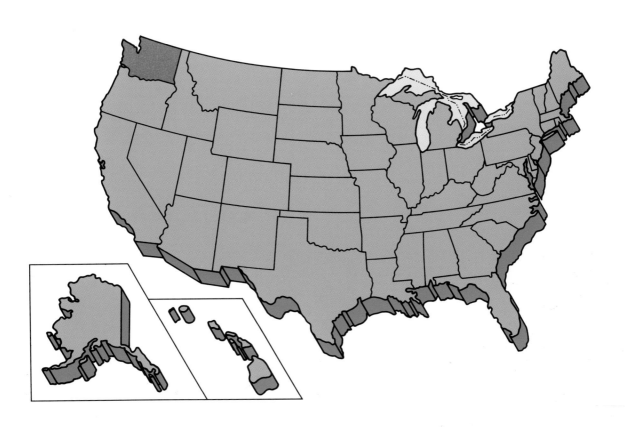

Hello U.S.A.

WASHINGTON

E. S. Powell

THE SEAL OF THE STATE OF WASHINGTON 1889

EAU CLAIRE DISTRICT LIBRARY
Lerner Publications Company

This book is available in two editions:
Library binding by Lerner Publications Company
Soft cover by First Avenue Editions, 1996
241 First Avenue North
Minneapolis, MN 55401
ISBN: 0-8225-2726-X (lib. bdg.)
ISBN: 0-8225-9738-1 (pbk.)

LIBRARY OF CONGRESS
CATALOGING-IN-PUBLICATION DATA
Powell, E. Sandy.
    Washington / E. S. Powell.
      p. cm. – (Hello USA)
    Includes index.
    Summary: Introduces the geography, history,
people, industries, and other highlights of the
Evergreen State.
    ISBN 0-8225-2726-X (lib. bdg.)
    1. Washington (State)–Juvenile literature.
[1. Washington (State)] I. Title. II. Series.
F891.5.P69 1992
979.7–dc20   92-13366

Manufactured in the United States of America
3 4 5 6 - JR - 01 00 99 98 97

Cover photograph by Jon Brunk.

The glossary that begins on page 68 gives definitions of words shown in **bold type** in the text.

This book is printed on acid-free, recyclable paper.

CONTENTS

Did You Know . . . ?

❑ Washington is the only state named for a U.S. president. The state takes its name from George Washington, the first president of the United States.

❑ On May 18, 1980, Washington's Mount Saint Helens erupted for the first time in 123 years, sending a plume of ash 11 miles (18 kilometers) into the air. The eruption covered some towns with as much as 7 inches (18 centimeters) of volcanic ash.

Washington's state flag sports George Washington on a green background, for the Evergreen State.

❑ Washington is one of the few states where you can still see hundreds of nesting bald eagles. This

6

awe-inspiring bird is an endangered species in most of the United States.

❑ As tall as a 46-story building, Grand Coulee Dam on the Columbia River in Washington is the largest concrete dam in the United States! It can light more homes than any other source of water-powered electricity in the country.

❑ In Washington some people claim to have seen Sasquatch, or Bigfoot. Legends of this huge, hairy, harmless creature have been passed down since Native Americans first lived in the region. But no one can say for sure if Bigfoot really exists.

A Trip Around the State

Washington—the Evergreen State—is known for its evergreen pine and fir trees. But only the lush western third of the state, from the Pacific coast to the Cascade Mountains, can truly be called evergreen. Most of Washington actually lies east of the Cascades. Here, rolling wheat fields and dry grasslands stretch mile after mile.

Bordering the Pacific Ocean in the northwestern corner of the United States, Washington belongs to the Pacific Northwest region of the country. Canada neighbors Washington on the north and the state of Idaho lies to the east. To the south, the Columbia River cuts much of the boundary between Oregon and Washington.

Washingtonians hold very different images of their state depending on whether they're from east *(above)* **or west** *(facing page)* **of the Cascade Mountains** *(inset).*

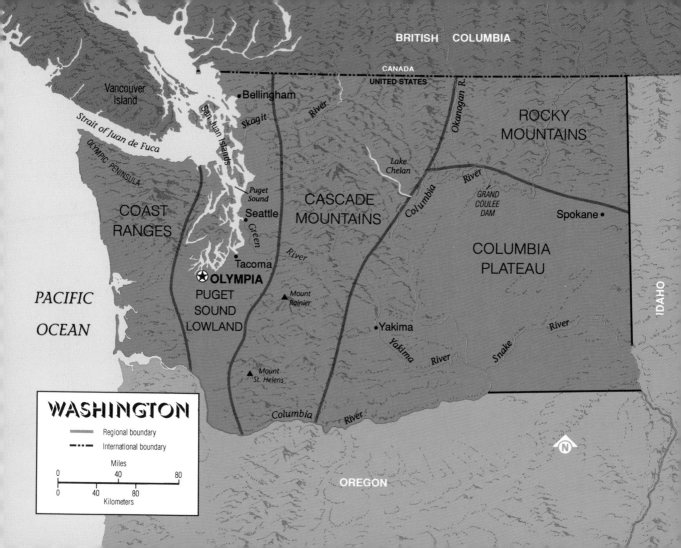

BRITISH COLUMBIA

CANADA
UNITED STATES

Vancouver Island

Strait of Juan de Fuca

OLYMPIC PENINSULA

San Juan Islands

Bellingham

Skagit River

ROCKY MOUNTAINS

Okanogan R.

Lake Chelan

Columbia

River

GRAND COULEE DAM

COAST RANGES

Puget Sound

Seattle

Green

River

CASCADE MOUNTAINS

Spokane

COLUMBIA PLATEAU

PACIFIC OCEAN

Tacoma

⭐ OLYMPIA

PUGET SOUND LOWLAND

▲ Mount Rainier

Yakima

Yakima River

Snake River

River

IDAHO

▲ Mount St. Helens

Columbia River

N

WASHINGTON

━━━ Regional boundary
━ ・ ━ International boundary

Miles
0   40   80

0   40   80
Kilometers

OREGON

More than 300 million years ago, the western coast of North America was near what is now Idaho. Over time, several smaller continents moved through the Pacific Ocean, pushing into and joining the larger North American continent. The smaller landmasses formed the land that is now Washington. As the landmasses hit North America, they rumpled into the mountains we see along the coast today.

Glaciers also helped shape Washington's varied landscape. When these huge sheets of ice melted, the sea level rose and water from the Pacific Ocean poured into the low spots that the glaciers had carved out. This is how the Strait of Juan de Fuca was formed. A narrow water passageway, the **strait** separates northwestern Washington from Canada's Vancouver Island.

Water also flowed south from the eastern end of the strait, creating Puget Sound. The deep, sheltered waters of Puget Sound have made this long inlet an excellent place to dock large ships for loading and unloading goods.

Washington can be divided into five geographic regions—the Coast Ranges, the Puget Sound Lowland, the Cascade Mountains, the Columbia Plateau, and the Rocky Mountains. The mountains of the Coast Ranges line the Pacific Ocean. The rugged northern section of the Coast Ranges juts into the ocean and is known as the Olympic Peninsula. To the south, the mountains are much lower.

Inland, a long valley stretches north from Oregon, curves around Puget Sound, and goes all the way into Canada. Called the Puget

Mist surrounds Cape Flattery, which forms the tip of the Olympic Peninsula.

The San Juan Islands are part of the Puget Sound Lowland.

Sound Lowland, this region is home to three out of four Washingtonians.

The scenic Cascade Mountains border the Puget Sound Lowland and rise as high as 14,410 feet (4,392 meters) at Mount Rainier. Several of these mountains were once active volcanoes. Washington's largest natural lake, Lake Chelan, lies in the Cascades. It was actually once a river, but glaciers blocked the flow of the river with soil and rock.

Washingtonians like to escape to the rugged beauty of the Cascade Mountains.

A hiker *(above)* enters the frigid air of a snow cave—a pocket formed when glacial snow melts near the earth's surface. Wheat fields *(above right)* roll across much of the Columbia Plateau.

East of the Cascades, glaciers also crossed the Columbia Plateau. When the glaciers started breaking up, they released huge floods of water that washed away the topsoil, leaving bare volcanic rocks called **scablands.** Only sagebrush and cheatgrass—plants that need little water and dirt—can grow in these areas. Gently rolling hills mark the **plateau,** a highland region.

Northeastern Washington rises into the Rocky Mountain region. From this corner of the state flows the mighty Columbia River, which curves 700 miles (1,126 km) through central Washington to the

The Okanogan River cuts through the Rocky Mountain region of northeastern Washington.

Pacific Ocean. The Okanogan River flows into the Columbia in northern Washington, and the Snake and Yakima rivers join the Columbia in the south.

Countless rivers and streams pour west out of the Coast Ranges and the Cascades, providing plenty of water for plants and animals. Many of these waterways, among them the Skagit and the Green, also supply water to the cities and towns of Puget Sound.

The climate in Washington depends on whether you're in western or eastern Washington. West of the Cascades the winters are mild. Summer days can top 90° F (32° C), with year-round rainfall around 60 inches (152 cm). The Olympic Peninsula gets as much as 180 inches (457 cm) of rain per year, creating one of the few **rain forests** in the United States.

Where rainfall is abundant, young Washingtonians can sail toy boats in puddles.

17

Wildflowers add splashes of color to Washington's countryside.

Winter in eastern Washington is colder, with much more snow than western Washington. Summers can be very hot and dry. Average rainfall on the Columbia Plateau is only 6 inches (15 cm) per year.

In all, more than half of Washington is covered with forests of Douglas fir, Sitka spruce, western hemlock, red cedar, and pine. Western Washington's woods have thick undergrowth. Eastern Washington, with its sparse forests, has one particularly unusual tree—the western larch. Although this tree has cones like other evergreens, its needles turn orange and drop off each fall.

The forests and lakes west of the Cascades provide homes for

marmots, otters, beavers, and countless other animals. Deer and elk live throughout the state. Grouse and pheasant are plentiful in eastern Washington. Oysters grow on the rocky beaches. And whales can be spotted off the coast.

A sea lion barks on Washington's coast *(right),* **while marmots play on a grassy hillside in the Cascades** *(above).*

Washington's Story

Long before Europeans came to what is now Washington, natural disasters struck the land. Although the events were tragic for the people who lived on the land, these disasters sometimes preserved clues that help modern people understand ancient life. When Mount Saint Helens erupted 3,500 years ago, the Indians, or Native Americans, who lived in the region must have fled. The only clues left about their life are ancient tools found buried under lava and ash.

Another big disaster happened sometime around A.D. 1500. Near Ozette on the Olympic Peninsula, a whole village was buried under a mud slide. When the village was discovered in 1970, buildings, skeletons, tools, sculptures, and baskets had all been perfectly preserved.

**Before Ozette was buried in mud,
Indians carved pictures into these rocks.**

20

The Makah Whalers

American Indians living along the Pacific coast depended on the sea for much of their food. But few groups undertook the life-threatening job of hunting whales. Among the daring were the Makah.

Whaling was a ritual for the Makah. To prepare for the hunt each spring, whalers and their wives fasted, bathed in hidden ponds, and recited secret prayers. Once a whale was spotted, the whalers would leave by canoe before dawn. Their wives would stay at home, lying perfectly still in the hopes that the whale would also be still.

The whaling crew paddled right up alongside the huge animal. They would wait until its head and tail were underwater so it couldn't flip or break the canoe. Then the lead whaler would plunge his harpoon into the whale's shoulder. The harpoon had a barbed tip that anchored into the flesh, and a long line with sealskin floats was tied to the other end of the harpoon. The floats slowed the whale, so it could not swim as far away.

Meanwhile, the crew paddled quickly backward to get away, and they began to sing songs to encourage the whale to swim toward shore. As the whale dove downward, the men tied on more lines with floats to slow the creature even more.

By the time the whale surfaced, other men had arrived in canoes to help throw more harpoons into the animal. After it died, a crew member would jump overboard to tie the whale's mouth shut. This kept water out of the whale's stomach, so it wouldn't sink.

The crew towed the huge carcass to shore, singing all the way. Villagers met them, welcoming the whale with songs and feasts.

Because of the Ozette mud slide, we know that the Makah Indians dug clams and hunted whales with wooden spears that were 18 feet (5.5 m) long. The sharp tips of the spears were made from mussel shells.

Other discoveries, as well as notes taken by the first white people to reach the area, have taught us about various groups of Indians in the Pacific Northwest. The way these different tribes lived depended on whether they were west or east of the Cascade Mountains.

West of the Cascades, tribes such as the Nooksack, Snoqualmie, and Snohomish made use of the abundant cedar trees. The houses in their villages were made from cedar. They pounded cedar bark to

During a potlatch, many coastal families gathered together for a huge feast and gift giving. The most honored chief gave away everything he owned.

be soft enough to make clothing. And they carved canoes out of cedar tree trunks.

For food, the western tribes caught salmon and other fish. They also gathered many edible

To prepare food for winter storage, Indian women hung fish on racks to dry in the sun.

plants from the dense forests. The roots of cattails and wapatoo, parts from lupines, thistles, and ferns, and many kinds of berries were all collected.

East of the mountains, the Yakima, Palouse, Spokane, and other groups lived along rivers. They traveled in spring and summer, searching for fresh fish, game, and berries. While these tribes were on the move, they set up portable lodges made from wood frames. Mats of woven grass were used to cover the frames. Travel became easier by about 1700, when the Palouse, Nez Percé, Cayuse, and others acquired horses by trading with tribes hundreds of miles to the south.

On the Columbia Plateau, women dried bitterroot in the sun *(right)*. The dried roots were stored in woven baskets *(inset)*.

In the winter, eastern tribes dug pits to make houses that were partially underground. Sometimes the houses were built next to cliffs, which blocked harsh winds. Clothing made from deer, elk, and bighorn sheep skins kept people warm. They ate fried cakes made from pemmican. This mixture of dried meat, fish oil, and dried berries lasted through the winter without spoiling.

25

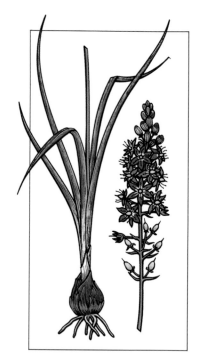

A favorite food for Indians on either side of the mountains was the camas lily bulb, which looks like an onion and tastes something like a sweet potato.

The Chinook, who lived near the Pacific Ocean along the mouth of the Columbia River, linked peoples west and east of the Cascades. They traveled upriver to trade shells and other valuable items with the families east of the mountains. For the most part, Native Americans in what is now Washington lived peacefully until white settlers began to arrive.

In the 1700s, Spanish, Russian, and British explorers sailed along the Pacific coast, making maps and trading with the coastal Indians. The Europeans bought the pelts of sea otters, beavers, and other animals and then sold them for a huge profit in China, where the furs were popular.

It wasn't until 1792 that Captain Robert Gray from Boston sailed along the coast of the Pacific Northwest. He made it through the rough waters at the mouth of the Columbia and named the river after his ship.

Long before Europeans discovered the Columbia River, Native Americans traveled the waterway to trade with other tribes.

That same year, George Vancouver from Great Britain explored the entire Washington coast and named several places—including Mount Baker, Mount Rainier, Puget Sound, and Whidbey Island—after his crewmembers. Vancouver also traveled up the Columbia and claimed the Pacific Northwest for Britain.

News of the Europeans' profitable fur trade reached the leaders of the United States. They paid two explorers, Meriwether Lewis and William Clark, to map a route from the Mississippi River to the Pacific Ocean. The last section of

A Shoshone Indian woman named Sacagawea helped guide the Lewis and Clark expedition. Without her help, the men might never have reached the Pacific coast.

Washington's early settlers met at Fort Vancouver to visit and to trade goods.

the route was to follow the Columbia River. Lewis and Clark's route made it possible for American and British settlers to travel to the Pacific coast by land as well as by sea.

In 1825 John McLoughlin, a British Canadian, established a trading post on the Columbia River. Called Fort Vancouver, the post encouraged white settlers to come to the region. Some of the first to arrive were mountain men who lived alone all winter, trapping in the mountains and coming together once a year to trade.

Other early settlers came with a mission of bringing the Christian religion to the Indians. These settlers were known as **missionaries**. In 1836 the missionaries Marcus and Narcissa Whitman settled among the Cayuse Indians in southeastern Washington.

At first the Cayuse got along with the Whitmans and other white settlers in the area. But then there was a serious misunderstanding. The Whitmans had been sharing their vegetables with the Indians. One day, the Whitmans put poison around their garden to kill the mice that were eating the vegetables.

When some Cayuse caught the measles and died, the Indians thought the Whitmans had purposely poisoned them, too. So the chief had the Whitmans and several other whites killed. Trust between the two groups was broken, and the mission was destroyed.

Narcissa Whitman

Marcus Whitman

Several other diseases brought by the settlers were also new to Native Americans and proved to be deadly. Cholera and smallpox took the lives of thousands of Indians. For example, just three weeks after disease broke out, only seven Indians were left in Wakanassi, a village near Fort Vancouver.

As more people from the United States and Britain settled in the Pacific Northwest, the two countries agreed to divide the land. The British moved their fur trading operations north from Fort Vancouver to Vancouver Island in Canada. This agreement left what was known as the Oregon Territory to be controlled by the U.S. settlers.

In 1853 the Oregon Territory was divided into the Washington and Oregon territories. The U.S. president appointed Isaac Stevens to be governor of Washington. Stevens convinced Indian tribes all over the territory to give up their claims to the land. In return he assigned them protected areas called **reservations**, where the Indians could live undisturbed by white settlers.

In 1855 Native American leaders met with Isaac Stevens to discuss a treaty.

The written agreement between Stevens and the Indians, called a **treaty,** gave the Indians two years to move. When Stevens began moving whole villages immediately, the Native Americans fought back. But they had been so weakened by disease that they couldn't defend their land. The Yakima and other tribes were angry, discouraged, and sick at heart as they moved onto reservations and discovered that their lives would be completely different.

While Indians mourned the loss of their land and way of life, white settlers poured in from the east. The thick forests west of the Cascades provided what seemed like endless opportunities for lumberjacks. Sawmills worked furiously to make timber for building. Towns near the sawmills soon grew into cities, particularly around Puget Sound. From these cities near the Pacific, lumber could be shipped to California, Hawaii, and even Australia.

Loggers found that Washington's forests had some of the world's largest trees.

Shipping became even more important in 1883, when the Northern Pacific Railway completed a cross-country line from the East Coast to Puget Sound. Some of the people who helped build the train tracks came from as far away as Asia.

By train, the journey between the East and West coasts was much easier than by covered wagon. The trains brought many more settlers to the territory. Before long it had enough people to apply for statehood, and in 1889 Washington became the 42nd state.

Besides lumber, the valleys west of the Cascades offered rich farmland, and fish were abundant. Life wasn't easy, though, since practically everything that people needed had to be homemade.

In the 1800s, fishers frequently caught salmon weighing nearly 100 pounds (45 kilograms). Since then, both the size and the number of fish have greatly declined.

The Little Town that Could

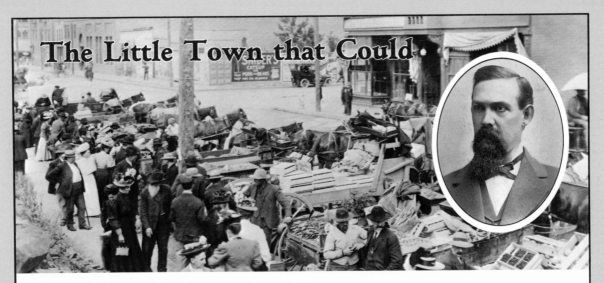

Towns sometimes grow up around the dreams and enthusiasm of a single person. Spokane, for instance, grew faster than any other city in Washington because of James Glover.

Determined to build a city he could call his own, Glover bought a sawmill in 1873. He was convinced that the spot was perfect for his dreams. Nearby Indians were friendly. Rich grasses grew in the area, and the falls of the Spokane River promised waterpower to generate electricity. Glover also believed that a railroad would eventually link Spokane with the country's East Coast and with Puget Sound. He encouraged others to settle nearby.

Even though the railroad took eight years to arrive, Glover's dream came true. In the 1880s the city became an important rail hub, and the population swelled with 5,000 newcomers each month.

35

Life in eastern Washington was even more difficult because of the cold winters and the long distances between homesteads. Wheat farming and cattle ranching were about the only ways to make a living. By 1890, though, ranchers began pumping water from nearby rivers to fields. Called **irrigation,** this process allowed people to grow fruit on the dry grassland.

Most people settled in the Puget Sound region because of the variety of work available. In the years around 1900, Seattle boomed, and shipbuilding became a major industry.

Washington gained fame as a state where people stood up for what they believed. Workers' organizations such as the Knights of Labor demanded fair wages and safe working conditions. Work in sawmills, for instance, was shortened from 12 to 10 hours a day.

Washington's industries grew

East of the Cascades, fruit growers dug irrigation channels to water their orchards.

Washington's shipbuilding industry grew rapidly in the early 1900s.

even more during the 1940s. The state's many ports made it a good place to build ships and aircraft to send overseas during World War II (1939–1945).

During this time, the Bonneville and Grand Coulee dams and the Hanford nuclear energy center were constructed. Each of these projects produced enough electricity to run machines in factories, and the dams also stored water from the Columbia River to irrigate fields.

Washingtonians disagree over whether these changes were positive. Some say Hanford, for example, has done more harm than good. During World War II, Hanford made ingredients for one of the two atomic bombs that were dropped on Japan. The bombs helped end the war, but Japanese survivors still suffer from the sickness caused by radiation from the bombs. Within Washington, residents are concerned about possible accidents at Hanford that could cause radiation to leak and harm people.

But the building of the Hanford plant and the two dams brought more jobs and money to the state. This was partly because **hydropower** (the electricity generated

During World War II, the U.S. government worried that some Japanese Americans might be spies for Japan. Hundreds of innocent Japanese Americans in Washington were sent to prison camps. Most lost their homes and their jobs.

by water from the dams) was cheap. It did not require any fuel such as coal or oil. Instead, it got its energy from the flow of a river's water. Thanks to hydropower, factories were built in Washington to make aluminum (a type of metal). In fact, Washington began to produce more aluminum than any other state.

After eight years of construction, workers completed Grand Coulee Dam in 1942.

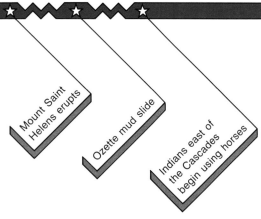

Mount Saint Helens erupts

Ozette mud slide

Indians east of the Cascades begin using horses

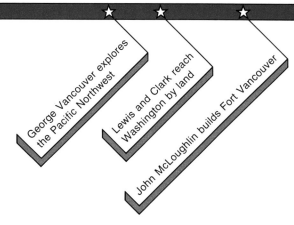

George Vancouver explores the Pacific Northwest

Lewis and Clark reach Washington by land

John McLoughlin builds Fort Vancouver

In the years since World War II, the state's population has grown rapidly as people move to Washington from other states, looking for better jobs and less crowded cities. New industries—including electronics and aerospace—have provided jobs for many of these people. And tourism has become another steady employer.

Tourists and Washingtonians alike value the state's ocean beaches, thick forests, rugged mountains, and open spaces. State and national parks throughout Washington preserve these natural areas. Residents are now discussing how to protect Washington's beauty and natural resources as more people move into the state.

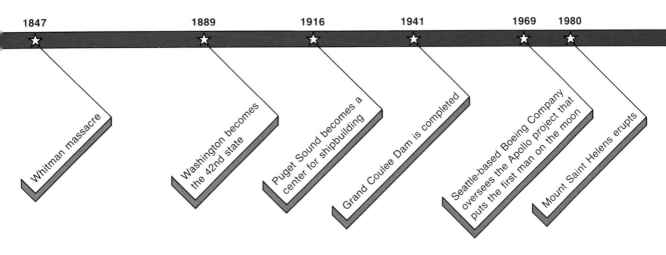

1847 Whitman massacre

1889 Washington becomes the 42nd state

1916 Puget Sound becomes a center for shipbuilding

1941 Grand Coulee Dam is completed

1969 Seattle-based Boeing Company oversees the Apollo project that puts the first man on the moon

1980 Mount Saint Helens erupts

Seattle is Washington's largest city. About three out of four Washingtonians live in cities.

Living and Working in Washington

By 1990 Washington's fast-growing population had nearly reached five million. Most of these people live in the Puget Sound area, which includes Seattle, Tacoma, and Olympia, the capital. Other cities include Bellingham in the north, Spokane in the east, and Yakima in central Washington. Recently, people have been moving away from the cities to areas such as the San Juan Islands, with their beaches and clean air.

From their roadside stand, a brother and sister sell chicken eggs to passersby.

43

Makah Indian drummers perform at a festival.

At one time, Native Americans were the only people living in the Pacific Northwest. Nowadays, about 81,000 Indians live in Washington. This amounts to less than 2 percent of the state's total population. But compared to the other 49 states, Washington's Native American population is large. In fact, it's the sixth largest in the country.

Other minority groups, including Asian Americans and African Americans, have made their homes in Washington, too. A variety of races and ethnic backgrounds is more likely to be found in the state's cities than in its small towns. Big cities often have more jobs and other opportunities for minorities.

Wearing colorful costumes, members of a Chinese marching team parade in Seattle's International District.

With the state's largest population, Seattle has many well-known museums—the Seattle Art Museum, the Pacific Science Center, and the Museum of Flight. The Burke Museum, also in Seattle, and the Museum of Native American Culture in Spokane offer a look into the Indian past.

Piglets nestle in straw at a county fair in northwestern Washington.

People flock to local arts-and-crafts festivals throughout Washington. A town's main street is often blocked to traffic so that craftspeople can display their work. County fairs are popular summer events too, featuring livestock pens and entertainment.

Washington residents and visitors enjoy hiking, fishing, boating, skiing, and camping in the state and national parks. Many Washingtonians like to mountain climb, and Mount Rainier is considered a perfect training ground for beginners and professionals alike. Windsurfers come from all over the world to take advantage of the strong winds in the Columbia Gorge. In professional sports, Washingtonians root for the SuperSonics basketball team and the Seahawks football team.

With 25 operating ferries, Washington has the largest ferry system in the United States. Each year, more than 19 million people ride the ferryboats. Many of the passengers are tourists

Mount Rainier towers over pleasure boats on a harbor in Puget Sound (above). **Young and old alike strive to the finish at a race during the Skagit Valley Tulip Festival** (left).

headed for the San Juan Islands and the Olympic Peninsula. Others are commuters, who depend on the ferries to get to and from work in Puget Sound.

Nearly one out of every six workers in Washington work in factories that manufacture a variety of products. Most of these people make airplanes, ships, and other transportation equipment. At the Boeing Company, the largest business in the state, thousands of workers produce airplanes and spacecraft. Boeing is one of the leading makers of commercial airplanes in the country.

Food processing, or the cleaning and canning of fish, berries, and vegetables, is the second most important type of manufacturing. Even salmon eggs, or roe, are carefully packed in salt and shipped to Japan. And Washington makes more computer software than most other states.

Many of Washington's products are shipped across the ocean to Asian countries that line the other side of the Pacific. Washingtonians who work in shipping and trade are called service workers because they perform a service for other businesses.

Some Washingtonians make parts to launch rockets into space.

Much of Washington's lumber is shipped to Pacific Rim countries on the Asian side of the Pacific Ocean.

More Washingtonians are involved in trade than in any other type of work. This is partly because Washington is closer to Asia than most other states are. Forest products, cars, chemicals, and foods are some of the products bought and sold.

Seattle is the second largest **containerport** in the United States. At the port's docks, huge containers—a whole train car or the rear of a truck—arrive full of goods such as electronic equipment, paper products, seafood, and apples. The containers are loaded onto ships that carry the goods across the Pacific Ocean.

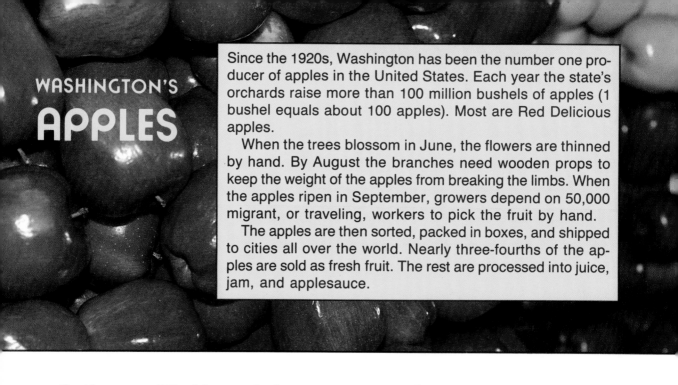

WASHINGTON'S
APPLES

Since the 1920s, Washington has been the number one producer of apples in the United States. Each year the state's orchards raise more than 100 million bushels of apples (1 bushel equals about 100 apples). Most are Red Delicious apples.

When the trees blossom in June, the flowers are thinned by hand. By August the branches need wooden props to keep the weight of the apples from breaking the limbs. When the apples ripen in September, growers depend on 50,000 migrant, or traveling, workers to pick the fruit by hand.

The apples are then sorted, packed in boxes, and shipped to cities all over the world. Nearly three-fourths of the apples are sold as fresh fruit. The rest are processed into juice, jam, and applesauce.

In the past, Washington's farmers grew a variety of crops on their land. But now farms have become more specialized, harvesting only one to three crops. Wheat, potatoes, and apples—all grown in the east—are some of the state's most important crops. Beef cattle graze on eastern ranches, and dairy cows thrive in the west.

For centuries, fishing has provided food for Indians in the Pacific Northwest. When Washington's white settlers began to fish to earn money, the supply of salmon and other fish seemed endless. But by the 1950s, Washingtonians began to realize that they could run out of fish.

Native Americans and white commercial fishers started fighting over who had the right to catch the state's shrinking number of salmon. In 1974 the courts ruled that Indians and whites had equal rights to the salmon. There are still hard feelings between the two fishing groups, but they are working together to leave enough salmon in Washington's waters for future generations.

Part of Washington's salmon catch is sold as smoked fish.

51

Logging has played a large part in Washington's history, bringing many people to the state. Some Washingtonians still depend on this industry to make their living. One-third of the trees cut each year are ground into pulp, which is then used to make paper products. At lumber mills, one-fourth of the logs felled each year are cut into boards. Much of Washington's lumber is shipped to Japan.

With its forested mountains and miles of coastline, Washington earns a lot of money from tourists. Like trade, tourism is a service industry because it provides services for people traveling through the state. Tourism sometimes turns disasters into money-makers.

For example, since the 1980 eruption of Mount Saint Helens, many tourists have come to the area. Visitors can view the crater and the devastation from sight-seeing planes and helicopters. Trinkets made of volcanic ash are sold at gift shops and grocery stores. In this way, Washingtonians are making the best of that disaster.

Fresh growth brings life back to Mount Saint Helens.

Protecting the Environment

Compared to some parts of the United States, Washington seems like a paradise. Mountain wilderness and long peaceful beaches grace western Washington, while the land and sky stretch endlessly east of the Cascades. Washington's natural beauty attracts tourists and helps create a variety of jobs. Many of the jobs depend on natural resources—trees for lumber, fish for food, and water for irrigation and electricity.

Some residents are concerned that industries are using up Washington's natural resources. Without these resources, many people could lose their jobs. Other Washingtonians fear for plants and animals when people change the environment. Together, these concerns show that the problems faced by plants and animals can signal problems for people, too.

Chinook salmon

In the 1800s and early 1900s, many people did not think that natural resources such as salmon would ever run out.

The story of Washington's salmon is a perfect example of how the lives of people and animals are interconnected. The fish begin their lives in freshwater streams hundreds of miles from the sea. As the salmon grow up, they swim to the saltwater ocean, where they will spend most of their adult lives. Just before they die, they return to their birthplace to spawn, or lay their eggs.

During their long journey to the ocean and back, the fish encounter many dangers. At their spawning grounds, the salmon cannot dig nests unless the water is a certain depth. When loggers cut down trees near rivers, soil slides easily down the bare banks into the water, bury-

Sockeye salmon prepare to spawn.

ing the spawning beds. Bad weather conditions, such as flooding and dry spells, can also change the depth of the water and prevent salmon from spawning.

When the fish do spawn, the baby salmon that hatch and survive swim downstream through farming areas. Farmers often spray their fields with poisonous chemicals to kill insects and make crops grow better. When it rains, the chemicals are washed into rivers, polluting the water and the fish.

Farmers also channel water from rivers to irrigate crops, lowering the water level in the streams. If the salmon live to make it farther downstream they face hydroelectric dams and polluted waters near towns and cities.

Irrigation sprinklers pump water from rivers.

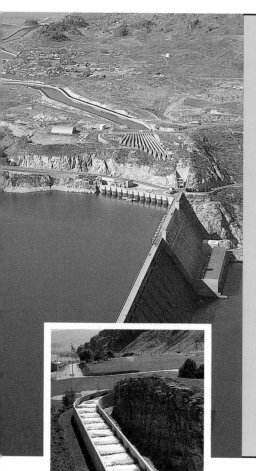

Deadly Dams

Hydroelectric dams seriously threaten the lives of salmon. When they head upriver to spawn, the salmon can't jump over the steep cement walls *(left)* of the dams. Fish ladders *(inset)* have been added so the salmon can climb the height of the dam one step at a time. But some fish don't find the ladders. Others die at the top because they get confused and lost in the slow-moving water of the reservoir, or artificial lake created by the dam. At each dam on the route, about one out of every ten salmon die.

Heading downriver, the young salmon, called smolts, run into even more problems from dams. The reservoir is warmer than the rest of the river, and some smolts die from over-heating or disease.

With so many dams along the way, the journey to the ocean takes much longer than it did before the dams were built. This gives predators such as bears and otters more time to prey on the smolts. The slower journey also means the salmon will not be able to adjust as well to life in salt water when they finally reach the ocean.

The engines that produce electricity at the dams can be deadly, too. Many of the smolts get caught and ground up in the blades of these engines. In all, three-fourths or more of all smolts die on the downriver journey because of dams.

Of those salmon that reach the ocean, many are netted by commercial fishers and sold to markets around the world. Although fewer and fewer salmon have been making it to the ocean each year, more and more have been caught.

Harm that comes to the salmon also affects other wildlife—wildlife that depend on salmon. Ducks and trout eat salmon eggs, and bears, otters, and bald eagles eat young salmon. At sea, salmon are food for dolphins, seals, and killer whales. Even plants depend on the nutrients they get from the salmon that die and decay along the mountain streambeds after spawning.

The numbers of salmon have dropped so drastically that some species, or types, have been added to the endangered species list. That means they are in danger of becoming extinct, and people must follow guidelines to save the salmon from dying out.

With amazing strength, salmon are able to leap up waterfalls on their journey to spawn. But dams are too high for the fish to scale.

Hatcheries—
Problem or Solution?

To help restore the numbers of salmon, people are now raising thousands of them in hatcheries. But hatchery fish are not as strong as wild fish. They are more likely to catch diseases and do not swim as well in rough water. Worse yet, when hatchery salmon breed with wild salmon, the weaknesses are passed on to the wild offspring.

The effort to save the salmon is touching nearly everyone in Washington. Fishers are having to catch fewer salmon. Farmers cannot use as much water for irrigation. Dams must have fish ladders. Power companies will have to use less water to create electric power. With less cheap hydroelectricity, homes and businesses will have to pay more for electricity.

For centuries, American Indians honored the salmon like a king. Saving this unique fish from extinction will not be easy. But Washingtonians could pay a much higher price by letting the salmon die out. People in the fishing and seafood-processing industries depend on salmon for their jobs. People who work in coastal towns depend on the money that sport fishers spend on their vacations. And some shipping companies earn money from transporting the salmon to markets. Washingtonians will have to work together to preserve the salmon that nourish so many animals, plants, and people throughout the state.

The future of
Washington's fishing
villages depends on the
future of salmon.

Washington's Famous People

ACTORS & MUSICIANS

Bing Crosby (1904–1977) was born in Tacoma. A popular singer and actor, Crosby starred in over 50 movies. His 1942 recording of the song "White Christmas" continues to be a bestseller.

Jimi Hendrix (1942–1970) is considered by some to be the best electric guitarist of all time. During his short career, he led a rock group called the Jimi Hendrix Experience and also performed solo. Hendrix grew up in Seattle.

Adam West (born 1938) played the role of Batman both in the 1966 film *Batman* and in the popular 1960s television series of the same name. West is from Walla Walla, Washington.

▼ JIMI HENDRIX

▲ ADAM WEST

ARTISTS

Minoru Yamasaki (1912–1986) was an architect from Seattle who designed more than 300 buildings. His most famous building is probably the World Trade Center in New York City.

George Tsutakawa (born 1910) grew up in Seattle and became a well-known sculptor. Some of his most famous sculptures are bronze fountains in parks in the United States and in Japan.

ASTRONAUT

Richard Gordon, Jr. (born 1929), piloted the *Gemini XI* space flight around Earth in 1966. In 1969 the astronaut flew the

62 ◀ MINORU YAMASAKI

Apollo XII spacecraft for the second landing on the moon. Gordon is from Seattle.

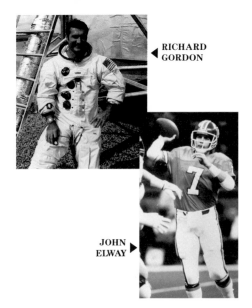

◄ RICHARD GORDON

ATHLETES

Earl Anthony (born 1938) is from Tacoma. As a professional bowler, he won 41 Professional Bowlers Association (PBA) tournaments and is a member of the PBA Hall of Fame.

John Elway (born 1960) is a quarterback for the Denver Broncos. Elway led his team to the Super Bowl game three times, and many football fans consider him one of the best quarterbacks in the National Football League. Elway is from Port Angeles, Washington.

James Whittaker (born 1929) was the first U.S. athlete to successfully climb Asia's Mount Everest, the world's highest peak. He has also reached the top of Washington's Mount Rainier 66 times. Whittaker is from Port Townsend, Washington.

JOHN ► ELWAY

◄ EDDIE BAUER

BUSINESS LEADERS

Eddie Bauer (1899–1986) of Orcas Island, Washington, was the first to make and sell winter coats quilted with goose down. The Eddie Bauer mail-order business, started in 1921, grew to include stores that sell a wide variety of outdoor gear and clothing.

William Henry Gates III (born 1955) began writing computer programs at the age of 14, before computers were widely used. In 1975 he started the Microsoft Corporation, which makes software for computers. Gates, who is sometimes called the King of Software, is from Seattle.

◄ BILL GATES

63

Chuck Jones (born 1912) from Spokane, Washington, developed the Looney Tunes and Merrie Melodies cartoons while working at Warner Brothers Pictures. Jones also created the cartoon characters Road Runner, Wile E. Coyote, and Pepe le Pew.

Hank Ketcham (born 1920) created the comic strip "Dennis the Menace," basing the main character on his son Dennis. The comic strip, first published in 1951, is now printed in more than 1,000 newspapers across the country. Ketcham is from Seattle.

Gary Larson (born 1950) of Tacoma, Washington, created the comic strip "The Far Side." The 1991 Cartoonist of the Year, Larson retired in 1995.

◀ GARY LARSON

◀ CHIEF SEATTLE

ENVIRONMENTAL & POLITICAL LEADERS

Denis Hayes (born 1944) organized the first Earth Day in 1970 and planned the first international Earth Day in 1990. Earth Day, celebrated yearly on April 22, is a day for people to learn how to keep the earth clean and safe for all living things. Hayes grew up in Camas, Washington.

Henry ("Scoop") Jackson (1912–1983) grew up in Everett and became a U.S. senator in 1953. Jackson supported the rights of minority groups and organized workers' groups. He also helped pass laws to conserve the use of energy.

Chief Seattle (1786?–1866), a wise and respected leader, was born on Puget Sound to a Duwamish mother and a Suquamish father.

◀ DENNIS HAYES

In his most famous speech, given in 1854, Seattle noted how quickly the land that the Indians had held for thousands of years would pass to white settlers.

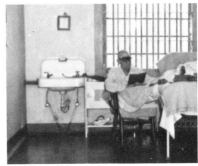

▲ ROBERT STROUD

PRISONER

Robert Franklin Stroud (1890–1963) of Seattle became known as the Bird-Man of Alcatraz. Stroud spent part of his 55-year prison term in Alcatraz, a former California prison. While serving his sentence, Stroud studied and cared for birds, becoming an expert in the field. He also earned college degrees in five different subjects.

FRANK ▶
HERBERT

◀ CAROLYN
KIZER

WRITERS

Barbara Helen Berger (born 1945) lives on Bainbridge Island, Washington. A children's illustrator and writer, she has won awards for her books, including *Grandfather Twilight, The Donkey's Dream,* and *Gwinna.*

Frank Herbert (1920–1986) created and wrote about science-fiction worlds described in *Dune* and other books. He won several science-fiction awards for his work. Herbert grew up in Tacoma, Washington.

Carolyn Kizer (born 1925) is a poet. In 1985 she won the Pulitzer Prize for her collection of poetry called *Yin: New Poems.* Kizer, of Spokane, Washington, is also the founder and editor of the magazine *Poetry Northwest.*

Facts-at-a-Glance

Nickname: Evergreen State
Song: "Washington, My Home"
Motto: *Alki* (an Indian word for "By and By")
Flower: coast rhododendron
Tree: western hemlock
Bird: willow goldfinch

Population: 4,866,692*
Rank in Population, nationwide: 18th
Area: 68,139 sq mi (176,480 sq km)
Rank in area, nationwide: 20th
Date and ranking of statehood:
   November 11, 1889, the 42nd state
Capital: Olympia (33,840*)
Major cities (and populations*):
   Seattle (516,259), Spokane (177,196), Tacoma
   (176,664), Bellevue (86,874), Everett (69,961)
U.S. senators: 2
U.S. representatives: 9
Electoral votes: 11

Places to visit: Old Fort Vancouver in Vancouver, Ape Caves near Mount Saint Helens, Hurricane Ridge in the Olympic Mountains, Rocky Reach Dam near Wenatchee, Palouse Falls in southeastern Washington

Annual events: Skagit Valley Tulip Festival (April), Bloomsday Run in Spokane (May), Toppenish Indian Pow Wow in Toppenish (July), Washington State International Kite Festival in Long Beach (Aug.), Wooden Boat Festival in Port Townsend (Sept.)

*1990 census

66

Natural resources: water, forests, soil, coal, gold, lead, zinc, clay, limestone, sand, gravel, fish and seafood

Agricultural products: wheat, potatoes, apples, cherries, plums, grapes, flower bulbs, dairy products, beef

Manufactured goods: airplanes, spacecraft, ships, food products, paper, lumber, wood chips, plywood, doors, shipping containers, chemicals, computer software

ENDANGERED SPECIES

Mammals—Columbian white-tailed deer, Townsend's big-eared bat, pygmy shrew, western gray squirrel

Birds—peregrine falcon, streaked horned lark, sandhill crane, white pelican, purple martin

Amphibians—Cope's giant salamander, Dunn's salamander, Larch Mountain salamander

Fish—Snake River sockeye salmon

Plants—Whited's milk-vetch, howellia, golden Indian-paintbrush, Washington polemonium, obscure buttercup

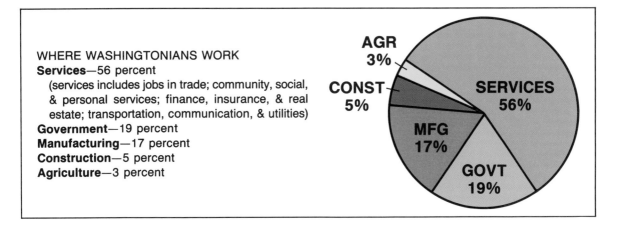

WHERE WASHINGTONIANS WORK
Services—56 percent
   (services includes jobs in trade; community, social, & personal services; finance, insurance, & real estate; transportation, communication, & utilities)
Government—19 percent
Manufacturing—17 percent
Construction—5 percent
Agriculture—3 percent

AGR
3%
CONST
5%
SERVICES
56%
MFG
17%
GOVT
19%

PRONUNCIATION GUIDE

Cayuse (KY-yoos)

Chelan (shuh-LAN)

Chinook   (shuh-NOOK)

Juan de Fuca (wahn duh FYOO-kuh)

Makah   (mah-KAW)

Nez Percé (NEZ PURS)

Palouse (puh-LOOS)

Puget Sound (PYOO-juht sownd)

Rainier (ruh-NIHR)

Seattle (see-AT-uhl)

Spokane (spoh-KAN)

Tacoma (tuh-KOH-muh)

Vancouver (van-KOO-vur)

Yakima (YAK-uh-maw)

Glossary

containerport A shipping port that is specially designed to handle cargo packed in large containers, such as train cars.

glacier A large body of ice and snow that moves slowly over land.

hydropower The electricity produced by using the force of flowing water. Also called hydroelectric power.

irrigation A method of watering land by directing water through canals, ditches, pipes, or sprinklers.

missionary A person sent out by a religious group to spread its beliefs to other people.

plateau A large, relatively flat area that stands above the surrounding land.

rain forest A thick, wet, evergreen forest with an annual rainfall of more than 100 inches (254 cm). Most rain forests are located in hot, wet climates near the equator. Washington has one of the few rain forests found in cooler climates.

reservation Public land set aside by the government to be used by Native Americans.

scabland Rocky land that was stripped of its soil when floods from melting glaciers washed away the soil.

strait A narrow stretch of water that connects two larger bodies of water.

treaty An agreement between two or more groups, usually having to do with peace or trade.

Index ▰▰▰▰▰▰▰▰▰▰▰▰▰▰▰▰▰▰▰▰▰▰▰▰▰▰▰▰▰▰▰▰▰▰

70

Acknowledgments:

Maryland Cartographics, Inc., pp. 2, 10; Jon Brunk, pp. 2–3, 14, 43, 46, 47 (both), 49, 51, 53, 61; Toby Schnobrich, p. 7; Kitty Kohout / Root Resources, p. 8; LINK / Visuals Unlimited, p. 9; Patrick Cone, pp. 9 (inset), 15 (right); Tore Ofteness, pp. 12, 13, 15 (left), 16, 20–21, 41, 57, 58; Doyen Salsig, pp. 17, 71; Jay A. Beck, p. 18; Diane Cooper, p. 19 (both); Special Collections Div., Univ. of Washington Libraries, pp. 23 (photo #NA703), 55, 64 (middle, Curtis #34127); Museum of History and Industry, pp. 24, 33, 34, 36, 37, 38; Burke Museum, p. 25 (inset, #25.0/145); Library of Congress, pp. 25 (right), 39; Kay Shaw, p. 27; Bryan Peterson, Legislative Media Services, p. 28; Oregon Historical Society, p. 29 (neg. #803); National Park Service, p. 30 (both); Washington State Historical Society, Tacoma, p. 32; Eastern Washington State Historical Society, p. 35 (both); © 1993 Adam Jones, p. 42; Jens Lund / Washington State Folklife Council, p. 44; Jim Corwin / AllStock, p. 45; Boeing Defense & Space Group, p. 48; Patricia Drentea, p. 50; Root Resources, p. 52; Oregon Department of Fish and Wildlife, p. 54; Will Troyer / Visuals Unlimited, p. 56; William J. Weber / Visuals Unlimited, p. 58 (inset); U.S. Dept. of Fish and Wildlife, Marvina Munch, p. 59; Ruth A. Smith / Root Resources, p. 60; Byron Crader / Root Resources, p. 69; TV Times, p. 62 (top right); Hollywood Book & Poster, Inc., p. 62 (middle left); Reprise Records, p. 62 (middle right); Taro Yamasaki / Daniel Bartush, p. 62 (bottom); NASA, p. 63 (top left); Independent Picture Service, p. 63 (top right); Eddie Bauer, Outdoor Outfitter, p. 63 (bottom left); Microsoft Corporation, p. 63 (bottom right); Universal Press Syndicate, p. 64 (top); Tony Russo, p. 64 (bottom); National Archives, p. 65 (top); Charles Brown, p. 65 (middle); Carolyn Kizer, p. 65 (bottom); Jean Matheny, p. 66.